DATE DUE

DEMCO 38-297

2003

*** NOTICE ***

IMPORTANT BILLING AND CREDIT REQUIREMENTS

All producers of the play *must* give credit to the author(s) of the play in all programs distributed in connection with performances of the play and in all instances in which the title of the play appears for purposes of advertising, publicizing or otherwise exploiting the play and/or a production. The name of the author(s) *must* also appear on a separate line, on which no other name appears, immediately following the title, and *must* appear in size of type not less than fifty percent the size of the title type. Biographical information on the author(s), if included in this book, may be used on all programs. *On all programs this notice must appear:*

"Produced by special arrangement with
THE DRAMATIC PUBLISHING COMPANY of Woodstock, Illinois"

THE HAPPY PRINCE was commissioned by the Kennedy Center for the Performing Arts.

THE HAPPY PRINCE

A One-act Play
For 3m., 5w., 2 either gender.
Or 4m., 4w. with doubling, plus extras.
Multicultural cast suggested.

CHARACTERS

THE HAPPY PRINCE
THE SWALLOW

TOWNSPEOPLE (2 men, 2 women and 2 children), who
play the multiple roles of:
    THE REED
    THE SEAMSTRESS
    THE LITTLE BOY
    THE PALACE BEAUTY
    THE PALACE LOVER
    THE PLAYWRIGHT
    THE LITTLE MATCHGIRL
    THE BEAUTIFUL ANGEL

PLACE: A city.

TIME: Now.

Approximate running time: 45 minutes

THE HAPPY PRINCE

TOWNSPEOPLE climb a hill, high above the city.

TOWNSWOMAN #1.
High above our sick and squalid city.

TOWNSMAN #1.
High above our sad and shallow city.

TOWNSWOMAN #2.
Our stinking city below, and on this verdant hill.

LITTLE BOY.
I want to see the statue.

LITTLE GIRL.
Me too.

TOWNSMAN #2.
On this beautiful hill, so green and lush.

TOWNSWOMAN #1.
We put all our hopes up here.

LITTLE BOY.
I want to see the statue.

TOWNSMAN #1.
We invested all our hopes right here.

TOWNSPEOPLE.
High above our stinking, smoking, smug city, stands
a magnificent statue.

TOWNSMAN #2.
We paid for it.

TOWNSWOMAN #2.
I designed it.

*(TOWNSPEOPLE gather for the unveiling. A cloth cover
hides the statue.)*

TOWNSPEOPLE.
On a tall, tall, tall column...

TOWNSMAN #1.
...reaching...

TOWNSWOMAN #2.
...yearning...

TOWNSMAN #2.
...straining to touch the heavens.

TOWNSMAN #1.
Gilt with thin leaves of fine gold.

LITTLE BOY.
I want to see the statue.

LITTLE GIRL.
Me too.

TOWNSWOMAN #2.
Eyes made out of two bright, shining green sapphires.

LITTLE BOY.
I want to see it. I want to see it NOW!

TOWNSWOMAN #1.
A golden statue to uplift us...

TOWNSMAN #1.
...to inspire us.

TOWNSWOMAN #2 *(puts her hand on the BOY's head)*.
...to bring us beauty.

(The cover is pulled to reveal—the HAPPY PRINCE, a golden statue encrusted with sparkling jewels.)

TOWNSPEOPLE.
THE HAPPY PRINCE! *(Beat.)* Aaaaaaahhhhhhhhhh.
Ooooooooooooooooohhhhhhhh.

LITTLE GIRL.
The prince looks like an angel!

LITTLE BOY.
   Teacher, are statues like angels on earth?
   Teacher, he does look like an angel.

TOWNSMAN #2.
   My dear boy, this *statue* is a beautiful representation
   of human endeavor, human ingenuity, a mixture of
   art and alloy. Metallurgical and mathematical. The x
   plus y of the arms and legs divided by the xx minus
   yy of the height and width and weight.

LITTLE GIRL.
   I think he looks like an angel.

LITTLE BOY.
   I saw an angel...in a dream. I was dreaming and I
   saw him. *(Points to the statue.)* It was for sure an
   angel.

TOWNSMAN #2 *(frowning, to TOWNSWOMAN #2)*.
   Madam, as a man of science, I disapprove of children
   ...dreaming.

TOWNSMAN #1.
   Well, I'm just glad there's someone in the world who
   looks quite happy. I, for one, am really miserable.

TOWNSWOMAN #1.
   A happy statue. Our money would have been better
   spent on something practical. A better landfill. We
   are drowning in our own garbage. Oh well, what's

the use of complaining. Here he is, the Happy Prince, beautiful as he is...useless.

LITTLE GIRL.
I bet the Happy Prince can talk to the moon.

TOWNSWOMAN #2.
Well, Timmy, time to go.

LITTLE BOY.
No, Mother! I don't want to go! I want to stay here and wait for the moon!

TOWNSWOMAN #2.
I said, let's go.

LITTLE BOY.
Nooooo. I want to wait for the moon. *(He drags his feet.)*

LITTLE GIRL.
Look, I think I see a star.

LITTLE BOY.
I see it, above the smokestacks.

TOWNSWOMAN #2.
Timmy, stop it. No stargazing. *(He cries.)* Stop it! Why can't you be more like the Happy Prince! You don't see him crying for anything. Look at him! *(He does.)* Do you see him crying for anything? Do you?

(The LITTLE BOY shakes his head.)

TOWNSMAN #1.
Young fellow, give your mom a big smile. A nice big smile, like this. *(Demonstrates, then sotto aside.)* I'm so miserable. *(To BOY.)* That's what I do when I don't get my way, and my wife hates me, and my boss keeps me from getting a promotion. When I feel like you do, I do this: *(Fake smile.)*

LITTLE GIRL.
I can smile too. *(Forces a smile.)*

TOWNSWOMAN #2.
Look, everyone is smiling except for you.

(Everyone plasters on a big wide fake smile. They exit.

Day turns to night. The stars and the moon appear and twinkle. A SWALLOW enters, mimes flying motions, circles above the cityscape.)

THE SWALLOW.
Where to land? Where to land? Smokestacks. Church steeples. Chimneys. My wings are tired. *(Circling again.)* Where to land? Where to land? Over here, by this golden tree. I will have a golden bedroom.

(The SWALLOW lands at the feet of the HAPPY PRINCE, who is weeping quietly.)

THE SWALLOW *(cont'd)*.
    This is just fine. Just tuck my head under my wing,
    and I'll be dreaming about my destination.

*(The following speech takes place with the SWALLOW
talking to the AUDIENCE from under its wing.)*

THE SWALLOW *(cont'd)*.
    That's where I'm going. A destination. A far-off
    destination! It's a long trip, my destination, I better
    get some sleep. *(Beat.)* What a curious thing? I feel a
    droplet. But not a single cloud in the sky. The stars
    are quite clear and bright. And yet... *(Another drop
    on the head.)* ...and yet it is raining. The climate
    here is truly dreadful. The Reed, my love, used to
    love the rain. But that was merely her selfishness!
    (Another drop, in the eye this time!) What is the use
    of a statue if it cannot keep the rain off? I'm going.
    (Sees the statue lit by the moon.) Wait. You are no
    ordinary statue. Your face...so beautiful in the
    moonlight. Who are you?

THE HAPPY PRINCE.
    I am the Happy Prince.

THE SWALLOW.
    Why are you weeping then? You have quite drenched
    me!

THE HAPPY PRINCE.
When I was alive and had a human heart, I did not
know what years were, for I lived in the Palace of
Sans-Souci, where sorrow is not allowed to enter.

THE SWALLOW.
I see. The Palace of Sans Souci, the Palace Without
Worry. That must have been nice. Never to worry. I
don't worry about much either, except when winter
comes.

THE HAPPY PRINCE.
Yes, winter is coming. It will be harsh this year, I
think.

THE SWALLOW.
I know. I was delayed. All my friends have flown to
Egypt, but my love, my heart, my beautiful reed
refused to come with me, she's a rather boring
conversationalist, but what do you expect from a
water weed.

(A river bank. THE REED, a beautiful water plant, appears in a vision.)

THE REED *(sings)*.
The river is my home, the only home
I've ever known.
You have travelled far and wide.
You have flown...so far.
Seen so much...but...
The river is my home, the only home

I've ever known.
This happy place, where I am grown.
How can I ever leave? Why must I go?
How can I leave? How can I go?
The answer, dear Swallow, is ... no.

THE SWALLOW.

I wanted to carry her away to Egypt, but she said no.
Still I loved her, and when all my friends departed
for warmer climates, I stayed with her as long as I
could. Winter is on my heels, but don't worry. I fly
like the wind. I fly faster than the wind.

(The PRINCE gazes out to the city, so melancholy.)

THE SWALLOW *(cont'd)*.

Please, don't be sad for me. I will forget all about my
sweet water flower, and soon, I will be soaring
among the pyramids of Egypt. Please, your tears
freeze upon your handsome face. Come now, let me
distract you. Tell me about a happier time. Tell me
about the Palace Without Worry. Must be nice, never
to worry.

THE HAPPY PRINCE.

In the daytime, I played games with my companions
in the garden, and in the evening, I led the dance in
the great hall. Round the garden, ran a very lofty
wall, but I never cared to ask what lay beyond it. Oh
dear Swallow. I never wanted to know what lay
beyond the palace walls. I gave grand parties, wore
beautiful clothes, and ate many sweet cakes.

THE SWALLOW.
  I see. Well, you were happy, and well-fed, that's all
  that mattered.

THE HAPPY PRINCE.
  My courtiers called me the Happy Prince, and happy
  indeed I was ... if pleasure and ignorance be
  happiness. So I lived, and so I died.

THE SWALLOW.
  You died?

THE HAPPY PRINCE.
  Yes, I died. Now I am dead, and made not of flesh
  and blood. I was bathed in gold and encrusted in
  sparkling gems. I am made of jewels, and gold leaf,
  and a heart made of lead.

THE SWALLOW (to AUDIENCE, aside).
  Lead? Not solid gold!

THE HAPPY PRINCE.
  They, the townspeople, have set me up here so high
  that, for the first time, I can see all the ugliness, and
  all the misery of my city ... and though my heart is
  made of lead ...

THE SWALLOW (to AUDIENCE, sotto).
  Lead, not gold.

THE HAPPY PRINCE.
  ... yet, all I can do is weep. I am so sad.

(A short silence.)

THE SWALLOW.
Well, I must be going.

THE HAPPY PRINCE.
Far away.

THE SWALLOW.
Yours is a sad story to be sure, but I must be going.

THE HAPPY PRINCE.
Far away in a little street, there is a poor house.

(The city. House of a SEAMSTRESS.)

THE HAPPY PRINCE *(cont'd)*.
One of the windows is open, and through it, I can see
a woman seated at a table.

*(We see the SEAMSTRESS and her bedridden LITTLE
BOY, racked by fever.)*

THE SWALLOW.
Where? I don't see this house. I don't see this
woman. I am not interested in the affairs of people.

THE HAPPY PRINCE.
O Swallow, look there. Her face is thin and worn,
and she has coarse red hands, all pricked by the
needle, for she is a seamstress.

SEAMSTRESS.
Look, Alexander. These are passion flowers.

LITTLE BOY.
So warm in here, Mother. I'm so warm.

SEAMSTRESS.
And this cloth, dearest Alexander, my Alexander, this
cloth is satin. *(Places the silk on his cheek.)* Feels
good. Feels cooling, soothing.

LITTLE BOY.
It's rough, and hot. I'm so thirsty.

SEAMSTRESS.
The queen's maid of honour will wear this satin
gown to the next court ball.

(The LITTLE BOY cries.)

LITTLE BOY *(muttering)*.
Mother ... Mother ... Mother ...

SEAMSTRESS.
Alexander, sweet Alexander ... you have a fever ...
calm yourself ... the fever will pass, I promise. Look
how beautiful ... these passion flowers. Let me distract
your fever with passion flowers.

LITTLE BOY.
Mother ... Mother ... I'm so thirsty.

SEAMSTRESS.
  I know you are warm, my darling. I know you are
  thirsty. I wish I had some oranges to give you.

LITTLE BOY.
  I like oranges.

SEAMSTRESS.
  I know you do, my darling. But there is no money
  for oranges. No money at all for food.

LITTLE BOY.
  I like oranges.

SEAMSTRESS.
  Come, let me distract your fever with a kiss.

THE HAPPY PRINCE.
  I can't bear it any longer. That poor child. That poor
  woman. That sweet child.

THE SWALLOW.
  Yes, too sad. Too bad. Well, I must go. I am waited
  for in Egypt. And it's far. Egypt is far.

THE HAPPY PRINCE.
  Little Swallow. Will you not bring her the ruby from
  my sword?

THE SWALLOW.
  I really must go and rest.

THE HAPPY PRINCE.
  I would go myself. But you see, my feet ...

THE SWALLOW.
  ... your feet?

THE HAPPY PRINCE.
  ... yes, my feet are fastened to this pedestal, and I
  cannot move.

THE SWALLOW.
  I see. Yes, I see that. Well, Prince ... Happy ... Happy
  Prince, I am waited for in Egypt. My friends, as we
  speak, are flying up and down the Nile River, and
  talking to the large lotus flowers. And soon, they will
  go to sleep in the tomb of the great king. The king
  himself is there in his painted coffin. Wrapped in
  yellow linen, and embalmed with spices. Round his
  neck is a chain of pale green jade, and his hands are
  like ... withered leaves.

THE HAPPY PRINCE.
  Please, little Swallow. Will you not stay with me for
  one night, and be my messenger? His mother is so
  sad, and the boy so thirsty.

THE SWALLOW.
  I don't much care for boys. Last summer, when I was
  staying on the river, there were two rude boys, the
  miller's sons, who were always throwing stones at
  me. They never hit me, of course, we swallows fly
  too fast for that. Throwing rocks at swallows is

disrespectful ... well ... it's getting very cold. Still ...
well ... all right. I will stay with you one night, and be
your messenger. But only this one night!

THE HAPPY PRINCE.
Thank you, little Swallow. Please take this ruby from
my sword, and give it to the child who so needs it.

THE SWALLOW.
I will. *(Beat.)* What's a ruby?

THE HAPPY PRINCE.
A ruby is a precious gem. Here on my sword.

THE SWALLOW.
I will remove this red ruby. I will do as you ask. It
doesn't want to come ... loose. *(To AUDIENCE.)* It's
very stubborn. Ah, I think ... I think ... I think ... I have
it.

*(The SWALLOW plucks the ruby from the sword. And
holds it aloft! The SWALLOW flies over the rooftops of
the city, until it alights on a wall near the palace.)*

THE SWALLOW *(cont'd).*
I smell food! I hear feet dancing. I hear the clinking
of glasses. And such beautiful music, and laughter
from such happy voices. Hm ... *(Looks around.)* This
must be the home of the prince, the Palace Without
A Single Worry.

(The palace. A balcony. A PALACE BEAUTY and HER LOVER stand gazing at the stars. MUSIC—a waltz or minute.)

PALACE BEAUTY.
How wonderful the stars are.

HER LOVER.
The stars are wonderful, but you are more sparkling than the entire night sky.

PALACE BEAUTY.
How wonderful the power of love.

HER LOVER.
I am in the grip of your power. Your love is making my heart, and my feet dance.

PALACE BEAUTY.
Oh silly, that's the music doing its work.

HER LOVER.
No, it's your face. Your beauty. Your open and kind heart.

PALACE BEAUTY.
My love.

HER LOVER.
My love.

PALACE BEAUTY.
  I can't wait for the state ball. It will be so lovely.

HER LOVER.
  You will be the loveliest flower there.

PALACE BEAUTY.
  I just hope my dress is ready in time. I ordered such
  a dress, oh my love. Wait until you see it. I am
  having passion flowers embroidered on silky cool
  satin. I just hope it's completed in time. Seamstresses
  are so lazy.

HER LOVER.
  They are, indeed! Very lazy!

PALACE BEAUTY.
  Look, there is a disgusting bird. Make it go away
  before it deposits something.

HER LOVER.
  Shoo! Shoo! I said, shoo!

PALACE BEAUTY.
  You heard him. Shoo!

  (House of the SEAMSTRESS. The SWALLOW arrives, tries
  to enter, but the SEAMSTRESS keeps waking.)

SEAMSTRESS (sleepily).
  And there will be so many oranges. Someday, all you
  can eat. (Almost nods off, but...) So many...so many

sweet, sweet, juicy oranges *(Nearly nods off.)* ...so
many ...

*(The LITTLE BOY, restless with fever; his MOTHER nods
to sleep.)*

THE SWALLOW.
I could put it here by her thimble.

LITTLE BOY *(muttering)*.
Mother...

(She nearly rouses.)

THE SWALLOW.
Perhaps I will put the ruby by the boy...she'll find it
there. I'll put it on his pillow.

LITTLE BOY *(muttering)*.
Mother...

THE SWALLOW.
This boy doesn't seem so terrible. He doesn't look
strong enough to throw stones at swallows. He's as
hot as the sun.

LITTLE BOY *(muttering)*.
Hot as the sun.

*(With his wing, the SWALLOW fans the LITTLE BOY.
The LITTLE BOY SIGHS with relief.)*

LITTLE BOY *(waking)*.
Am I going to die?

THE SWALLOW.
No, you are not. You will live to play and sing, and
to tell other little boys not to throw stones at any
living thing with wings. Sleep. Sleep. Sleep.

(The SWALLOW sings; fans the LITTLE BOY.)

THE SWALLOW *(sings)*.
You will play and sing another day.
You will look at swallows in a special way.
Tell little friends to lay down their stones.
Tell little friends to admire flight. Right? Right!.
Dance and drink cool shade and breezes.
Eat sweet oranges! And fly, no sneezes!
Play and sing, and laugh all the day,
Fly kites, sing songs, eat sweet oranges! Right? Right!
Fly kites, sing songs, eat sweet oranges! Take flight.

*(Night turns into day. The TOWNSPEOPLE gather about
the HAPPY PRINCE.*

*Meanwhile, at the SEAMSTRESS' house, the following is
enacted:)*

TOWNSMAN #1.
The seamstress found the gleaming red ruby.

TOWNSWOMAN #1.
  She chased a small white swallow out of her sick
  boy's bed.

LITTLE BOY.
  I feel much better.

LITTLE GIRL.
  And he ate two oranges!

TOWNSMAN #2.
  The seamstress chased the swallow.

LITTLE BOY.
  Around and around and around the room.

TOWNSMAN #1.
  ... into corners ...

LITTLE GIRL.
  He threw an orange peel. Watch out!

TOWNSWOMAN #1.
  ... up to the ceiling, until ...

TOWNSPEOPLE.
  ... she grabbed her broom, and gave the swallow a
  good whack.

THE SWALLOW.
  She knocked me right out the window.
  And tumbling and hurtling and falling I go.

(Sound of a COCK CROW.)

TOWNSPEOPLE.
Time to go! Time to go to work! *(They exit.)*

(The SWALLOW lands at the HAPPY PRINCE's feet.)

THE HAPPY PRINCE.
There you are. I was worried about you.

THE SWALLOW.
I was worried about me too. That seamstress has very
good aim. *(Rubs his sore backside.)*

THE HAPPY PRINCE.
The little boy is better now. His mother found the
ruby, and she bought eggs and cakes and oranges...
and a shop for her work.

THE SWALLOW.
It is curious.

THE HAPPY PRINCE.
What is curious, my friend?

THE SWALLOW.
Well, I feel quite warm now, although it is quite cold
this morning.

THE HAPPY PRINCE.
That is because you have done a good deed.

THE SWALLOW.
 I did?

THE HAPPY PRINCE.
 Yes, you did.

THE SWALLOW.
 Yes, I did. A good deed. *(Beat.)* I feel so warm, I
 think this would be a good time to continue on with
 my journey. I have a destination!

THE HAPPY PRINCE.
 Yes, I know. Now the day is nearly as cold as the
 night.

THE SWALLOW.
 I think even the moon shivers from the chill.

THE HAPPY PRINCE.
 Little Swallow, will you not stay with me one day
 longer? Far across the city, I see a young man in a
 cold stark room.

(We see the SWALLOW's following vision of Egypt.)

THE SWALLOW.
 But I am waited for in Egypt. Soon my friends will
 fly up to the Second Cataract. The riverhorse
 crouches there among the bulrushes, and on a great
 granite throne sits the god Memnon. All night long
 he watches the stars, and when the morning star

shines he utters one cry of joy, and then he is silent. I really must go and listen to such magnificent silence!

THE HAPPY PRINCE.
The young man is leaning over a desk, covered in papers, and in a tumbler by his side, there are stems from withered flowers.

(Egypt fades and changes to an attic with a large torn hole in the roof. We see the PLAYWRIGHT as described by the PRINCE, at his desk, writing.)

THE HAPPY PRINCE *(cont'd).*
Sad withered flowers.

THE SWALLOW.
I think they are roses. *(Peers closer.)* No, I believe, they are violets.

THE HAPPY PRINCE.
Yes, I believe you are right, little Swallow. Perhaps from an opening night. The young man is trying to finish a play for the director of the theatre. He is a scribe, a playwright, writer for the stage, but he is too cold to write anymore.

THE SWALLOW.
His hair is brown and crisp. His lips are red as pomegranate. He has large, and dreamy, and *red* eyes. What's wrong with the young fellow?

THE HAPPY PRINCE.
There is no fire in the grate, and hunger has made
him faint.

THE SWALLOW.
He is sad.

THE HAPPY PRINCE.
He is.

THE SWALLOW.
I will stay with you one day longer.

(The PRINCE and SWALLOW regard each other.)

THE SWALLOW *(cont'd).*
Shall I take him another ruby?

THE HAPPY PRINCE.
Alas, little Swallow. I have no ruby now. *(A short
pause.)* My eyes. My eyes are all that I have left.
They are made of rare sapphires, which were brought
out of India a thousand years ago. Pluck out one of
them, and take it to him.

THE SWALLOW.
No, I cannot pluck out your eye. Only you can see
from such magnificent eyes.

THE HAPPY PRINCE.
Take it to him. He can sell it to the jeweller, and buy
firewood, and finish his play.

THE SWALLOW.
Dear Prince, I cannot do that. *(SWALLOW weeps.)*

THE HAPPY PRINCE.
Swallow, Swallow, little Swallow.

THE SWALLOW.
No, don't ask me to do this.

THE HAPPY PRINCE.
My friend, pluck out my eye. Do as I ask you.

THE SWALLOW.
I should have left for Egypt, then I would not be
taking from your beautiful eyes.

THE HAPPY PRINCE.
Little Swallow, my friend. Little Swallow, my friend.

PLAYWRIGHT.
What's the use? No one wants this drivel. These
papers are better off in the fire. *(The PLAYWRIGHT
crumples his papers, sweeps them onto the floor, and
puts his head in his hands.)*

THE SWALLOW.
The playwright is dead?

THE HAPPY PRINCE.
No, just unappreciated.

THE SWALLOW.
   That is like being dead.

THE HAPPY PRINCE.
   Yes, it is.

THE SWALLOW.
   I will go to him.

   (The HAPPY PRINCE smiles.)

PLAYWRIGHT.
   The draft from the roof is unbearable. The chill goes
   straight to the bone. These papers are ridiculous. No
   one cares to hear a story anymore. I should put them
   where they will do more good. This page. *(To the
   page.)* Should you feed the soul, or will you serve
   better purpose feeding the fire.

   *(The SWALLOW flies into the room and perches on the
   roof.)*

PLAYWRIGHT *(cont'd).*
   I can't do it anymore. To what end? When audiences
   long to be lulled, to be comforted by the easy and the
   known. But you take them into unknown territories,
   and for this I am despised. *(To page.)* I despise you. I
   have had enough of you. *(He buries his head in his
   hands again.)*

THE SWALLOW.

I think this roof is very unstable. *(The SWALLOW mimes falling and tumbling into the room.)* This playwright must be hard-of-hearing, or very deep in his despair.

PLAYWRIGHT.

What is the use?

THE SWALLOW.

He doesn't move when he hears a clatter. *(The SWALLOW trips on the scattered papers.)* Perhaps, he is too familiar with falling tiles and howling winds through that growing hole! I'll put the sapphire here, by his noble head. Poor playwright. *(The SWALLOW peers at the PLAYWRIGHT closely and then sets the gem down.)* Poor, poor, poor playwright. A low and wretched person, made low by indifference and mediocrity of stubborn lazy minds. A gift for you from the Happy Prince, your patron.

(The SWALLOW leaves, flies out the roof, sending another tile CRASHING. The PLAYWRIGHT looks up. Sees the gem, holds it to the light. It's gleaming!

TOWNSPEOPLE, doing chores around town, stop and address the AUDIENCE.)

TOWNSMAN #1.

I heard the playwright finished his play, it will have a magnificent opening night!

TOWNSWOMAN #1.

   He told me a generous patron appreciated his work
and gave support to his efforts.

LITTLE GIRL.

   He laughs a lot now. I like that.

TOWNSWOMAN #2.

   The poor man hadn't eaten in a week, except old
dried bread crusts and stale river water.

TOWNSMAN #2.

   Now, he feasts on funnel cake and shares his bread
with friends, artists all. And most importantly, he is
writing, writing, writing.

LITTLE BOY.

   And laughing too.

LITTLE GIRL.

   I like the way he laughs.

TOWNSPEOPLE.

   He laughs way too much. Art should be serious!

*(Day turns into night. The SWALLOW is at the shoulder
of the HAPPY PRINCE.)*

THE SWALLOW.

   I am come to bid you goodbye.

THE HAPPY PRINCE.
Swallow, Swallow, little Swallow.
Stay with me one night longer.

THE SWALLOW.
It is nearly winter. The chilling snow will soon be
here. In Egypt, the sun is warm on the green palm
trees, the crocodiles lie in the mud and look lazily
about them.

(Again, a vision of Egypt.)

THE HAPPY PRINCE.
In the square below ...

*(A city street. A LITTLE MATCHGIRL near a lamplight.
She is on her knees, picking up scattered matches from
the gutter.)*

THE SWALLOW.
My companions must now be building a nest in the
Temple of Baalbek, and the pink and white doves are
watching them, and cooing to them and to each
other. Dear Prince, I must leave you, but I will never
forget you.

THE HAPPY PRINCE.
In the square below, there stands a little matchgirl.
Do you see her?

THE SWALLOW.

Dear Prince, next spring when I return, I will bring you back two beautiful jewels to replace those you have given away so freely. This new ruby shall be redder than a red rose, and the sapphire shall be as blue-green as the great blue-green sea.

THE HAPPY PRINCE.

In the square below, there is a little matchgirl. She has let her matches fall in the gutter, and they are all spoiled. Her father will beat her if she does not bring home some money, and she is crying.

THE SWALLOW.

I see her, but, dear Prince, I must go.

THE HAPPY PRINCE.

The girl has no shoes or stockings, and her little head is bare. Pluck out my other eye, and give this gem. If you do this, her father will not beat her.

THE SWALLOW.

Dear Prince. That I cannot bear to watch. But I cannot pluck out your other eye, for then you would be quite blind.

THE HAPPY PRINCE.

Take the sapphire.

THE SWALLOW.

You break my heart, dear Prince. But I will do what you ask of me, because I know it makes you happy.

LITTLE MATCHGIRL.
My father will be so angry with me. All of them are
ruined. *(Picks up a match, holds it up.)* None can be
saved. Father will beat me and give me no supper.

*(The SWALLOW flies to the LITTLE MATCHGIRL and
plays with her—at first she doesn't want to play tag.)*

THE SWALLOW.
Try to catch me.

LITTLE MATCHGIRL.
Go away, can't you see I'm busy?

THE SWALLOW.
Try to catch me.

LITTLE MATCHGIRL.
I am busy here. Look, how clumsy I am. If I pick
them all up and dry them, perhaps they might still
sell.

THE SWALLOW.
Forget it. They are too wet.

LITTLE MATCHGIRL.
You are right, they are too wet and muddy.
No one will buy them now.

THE SWALLOW.
Catch me.

(Soon, the antics of the soaring, swooping SWALLOW make her laugh.)

LITTLE MATCHGIRL.
What a funny bird. Silly thing. This is a grave situation. My father will beat me. See, I have spilled the basket and now I cannot sell these matches. They are spoiled now, all wet. Silly thing, you want me to catch you? I would like to stroke your head, and your feathers, and ask you to teach me how to fly away.

THE SWALLOW.
Yes, I will teach you to fly and you can go with me to Egypt! But first a gift. Hold out your hand! *(The SWALLOW gives her the gem.)*

LITTLE MATCHGIRL.
What a lovely bit of glass! It sparkles and dances so in the lamplight. It makes me smile and laugh. I must show it to Father. *(She laughs gaily, exits.)*

(TOWNSPEOPLE wear scarves which are billowing from a strong HOWLING WIND.)

TOWNSMAN #1.
The wind says winter is coming.

TOWNSWOMAN #1.
A northern wind from unkind places.

LITTLE BOY.
Swirling ribbon ...

LITTLE MATCHGIRL.
  ...of cold air.

TOWNSMAN #2.
  A cruel wind.

TOWNSWOMAN #2.
  A bleak zephyr.

TOWNSMAN #1.
  An unkind gust.

TOWNSWOMAN #1.
  A wind with an iron grip.

TOWNSWOMAN #2.
  Bringing winter.

LITTLE BOY.
  I'm so cold.

LITTLE MATCHGIRL.
  I'm so cold.

TOWNSPEOPLE.
  We are all so cold!

(The SWALLOW is beleaguered by the strong WIND, finally makes it to the HAPPY PRINCE.)

THE HAPPY PRINCE.
   I heard that the little matchgirl now wears a coat and
   a warm scarf about the neck, and her father does not
   beat her, he kisses her for finding such a sapphire
   that so changed their fortunes.

THE SWALLOW.
   You are blind now.

THE HAPPY PRINCE.
   This is true.

THE SWALLOW.
   I will stay with you.

THE HAPPY PRINCE.
   No, little Swallow. You have stayed too long. I have
   been too selfish keeping you.

THE SWALLOW.
   It was my choice to stay.

THE HAPPY PRINCE.
   Winter is here, and you must go away to Egypt,
   where your friends await you in the sun.

THE SWALLOW.
   No, I will stay with you. Let me tell you stories of
   what I have seen in strange lands.

   (Night turns to day.)

THE SWALLOW *(cont'd).*
  Red ibises, strange birds, who stand in long rows on
  the banks of the Nile, and catch goldfish in their
  beaks.

  (Day turns to night.)

THE SWALLOW *(cont'd).*
  And the sphinx is a wonder, Dear Prince. The sphinx
  is as old as the world itself, and lives in the desert,
  and knows everything.

  (Night turns to day.)

THE SWALLOW *(cont'd).*
  I have seen merchants who walk slowly by the side
  of their camels and carry amber beads in their hands.

  (Day turns to night.)

THE SWALLOW *(cont'd).*
  I have met the king of the Mountains of the Moon,
  who are as black as ebony and who worship a large
  crystal. There, a great green snake sleeps in a palm
  tree, and has twenty priests to feed it with
  honeycakes. And there are pygmies too, who sail
  over a big lake on large flat leaves, and who are
  always at war with the butterflies.

THE HAPPY PRINCE.
  Dear little Swallow. You have told me over many
  days and nights, so many marvellous things, but to

tell you truly, nothing is more marvellous than my
own city. You have been to Egypt, but I would rather
hear what you see when you fly over my city, little
Swallow. Tell me what you see.

*(The SWALLOW hops down from his perch, and at stage
center, mimes flying, and describes the TOWNSPEOPLE
he sees:)*

THE SWALLOW.
Dear Prince. I see the wealthy and the rich with their
gold and silver coins stacked on tables. I see the
wealthy and rich making merry in their beautiful
homes, while ragged beggars sit outside their gates.

TOWNSWOMAN #1.
The swallow flew into dark alleyways.

TOWNSMAN #1.
And saw the hungry children.

LITTLE BOY.
I am so hungry.

LITTLE MATCHGIRL.
Will you buy a match? Buy a match, please.

LITTLE BOY.
I'm so hungry.

THE SWALLOW.
Dear Prince, I see two little boys under an archway
of a bridge, two little children huddling together in
each other's arms to keep themselves warm.

TOWNSWOMAN #2.
So many children with no place to live.

TOWNSMAN #1.
So many children with no food to eat.

TOWNSWOMAN #1.
So many children doing without.

LITTLE BOY.
No one loves us.

LITTLE MATCHGIRL.
No one loves me.

THE HAPPY PRINCE.
Dear Swallow, little Swallow, you are my feet and
my eyes. I cannot hear anymore. I am covered with
fine gold. You must take it off, leaf by leaf, and give
it to my poor children; the living always think gold
can make them happy.

THE SWALLOW.
This gold will give warmth to your people, so I will
do it, dear Prince.

(The SWALLOW distributes warm articles of golden clothing to the TOWNSPEOPLE.)

THE SWALLOW *(cont'd)*.
Leaf after leaf, I took small pieces of gold.

LITTLE MATCHGIRL.
In his beak!

THE SWALLOW.
Leaf after leaf, I carried small pieces of gold.

LITTLE BOY.
I have a coat!

LITTLE MATCHGIRL.
I have gloves and a pretty hat!

THE SWALLOW.
Leaf after leaf, I took small slivers of gold.

LITTLE BOY.
We have bread now!

THE SWALLOW.
Leaf after leaf, I took small fingers of gold.

LITTLE MATCHGIRL.
I have a blanket now!

THE SWALLOW.
Leaf after leaf of gold.

TOWNSMAN #1.
I have a winter hat.

TOWNSWOMAN #2.
We have winter gloves to warm our freezing hands.

LITTLE BOY.
And oranges, and meat...

LITTLE MATCHGIRL.
... and milk!

(Snow begins to fall on the SWALLOW, TOWNSPEO-PLE.)

TOWNSPEOPLE.
Then the snow came, and after the snow came the frost. Then more snow. And more snow. And more snow.

TOWNSMAN #1.
The streets looked as if they were made of silver.

TOWNSWOMAN #1.
The streets so bright and glistening.

TOWNSMAN #2.
Long icicles.

TOWNSWOMAN #2.
Like crystal daggers.

LITTLE BOY.
Long icicles hung down like crystal daggers...

LITTLE MATCHGIRL.
... from the eaves of all the houses.

THE SWALLOW.
Everybody went about their business.

TOWNSMAN #1.
In a fur coat.

THE SWALLOW.
Going to work.

TOWNSWOMAN #1.
In a fur coat.

THE SWALLOW.
Going to homes of friends.

LITTLE BOY.
And going to the pond to skate on the ice with a
brand-new hat.

LITTLE MATCHGIRL.
Skating? Let's go!

THE SWALLOW.
Going to their factories, their hospitals, their
bakeries, their churches, their offices, their theatres in
coats and jackets made of fur.

(The SWALLOW returns to the HAPPY PRINCE.)

TOWNSPEOPLE.
We were all warm. All of us were warm, except for the prince and the swallow.

THE SWALLOW.
All of them never knew what the Happy Prince had sacrificed for them. *(To PRINCE.)* Goodbye, dear Prince.

THE HAPPY PRINCE.
I am glad you are going to Egypt at long last, little Swallow. You have stayed too long here, and winter is settling in for a long sleep over my city.

THE SWALLOW.
May I kiss your hand in fond farewell?

THE HAPPY PRINCE.
Little Swallow, you must kiss me on the lips, for I love you. And when you go to Egypt, I will love you still.

THE SWALLOW.
It is not to Egypt that I am going, dear Prince. I am bound for another destination.

(The SWALLOW kisses the HAPPY PRINCE, and then, the SWALLOW falls dead at the PRINCE's feet. A long pause.

One by one, TOWNSPEOPLE in their fur coats enter and gather at the statue.)

TOWNSMAN #1.
Dear me! How shabby the Happy Prince looks.

TOWNSWOMAN #2.
How shabby, indeed! This was not supposed to happen. We used the best materials.

TOWNSMAN #2.
Someone has vandalized it.

TOWNSWOMAN #2.
It's absolutely ruined.

LITTLE BOY.
It's ugly.

LITTLE MATCHGIRL.
He's ugly.

TOWNSMAN #1.
Hideous.

TOWNSWOMAN #2.
The ruby has fallen out of his sword.

LITTLE BOY.
He has no eyes.

LITTLE MATCHGIRL.
He scares me.

TOWNSMAN #1.
The sapphires in his eyes are gone.

TOWNSWOMAN #2.
He's no longer golden.

LITTLE MATCHGIRL.
He doesn't look like an angel.

TOWNSMAN #2.
He's more miserable than I am. That's not very inspiring.

TOWNSWOMAN #2.
He's depressing. And not very useful anymore to anyone.

LITTLE BOY.
He looks like a beggar.

TOWNSMAN #1.
He looks like a bum.

(A BEAUTIFUL ANGEL appears.)

LITTLE BOY.
There's a dead bird at his feet!

LITTLE MATCHGIRL.
A dead bird!

TOWNSPEOPLE.
A dead bird, disgusting!

TOWNSMAN #1.
We must really issue a proclamation, birds must not be allowed to die here.

TOWNSWOMAN #2.
That's right, it's depressing.

TOWNSMAN #2.
And a health hazard.

LITTLE BOY.
He's all cold and stiff.

TOWNSWOMAN #2.
Don't touch it!

TOWNSMAN #1.
The statue should be torn down.

TOWNSWOMAN #2.
Disinfect it.

TOWNSMAN #2.
Burn it.

TOWNSMAN #1.
We must have another statue, of course, and this
time, I think it should be a statue of myself. *(ALL
TOWNSPEOPLE look at him in disgust.)* Yes, of
myself, and why not?

TOWNSPEOPLE.
Why not?

TOWNSMAN #2.
Why not a statue of me?

LITTLE BOY.
Or of me.

TOWNSWOMAN #2.
Or of me.

LITTLE MATCHGIRL.
What about me?

*(They all argue amongst themselves, making a nasty ca-
cophony of NOISY ARGUMENT.)*

BEAUTIFUL ANGEL.
And God bade me to come to earth, and to find the
two most precious things in this sad and squalid city.

TOWNSMAN #2.
We tore down the statue.

TOWNSWOMAN #2.
We melted it down in a hot and fiery furnace.

LITTLE MATCHGIRL.
We threw the dead bird away. I found a strange heart
made of lead. The heart was cracked in two.

LITTLE BOY.
I saw the heart, it was made of lead, and it was
broken. The heart was broken.

TOWNSPEOPLE.
We took the broken heart and threw it away. And
there, it lay next to the dead bird. The broken heart
of lead, and the cold dead bird.

BEAUTIFUL ANGEL.
And when God asked to see the two most precious
things on earth...

... I went into a sad and shallow city, below a
snow-covered hill, and there, I came upon a pile of
sad and bent and twisted rubble.

I bent down and with my angel's hand, I bent down
and scooped up a broken lead heart, a lead heart it
was, cracked into two... and the body of a small bird,
a swallow.

And God said to me, You have rightly chosen. God
spoke and said, You have chosen rightly.

(The BEAUTIFUL ANGEl ascends toward heaven. She takes the SWALLOW and the PRINCE with her.)

TOWNSPEOPLE.
You have rightly chosen. For in my garden of earthly Paradise, this little bird shall sing forever. This humble little bird will sing to God forever.

And in my city of gold, the Happy Prince shall smile and praise me. The Happy Prince will laugh and smile ... forever.

(The entire stage is overcome by a field of bright and twinkling stars.)

BLACKOUT

END OF PLAY

DIRECTOR'S NOTES

DIRECTOR'S NOTES

DIRECTOR'S NOTES